ISBN: 9798871365885

Copyright ©2023 Tortured Soul With A Pen. All rights reserved.

This book or any portion thereof may not be reproduced or used in the manner whatsoever without the express written permission from the publisher except for the use of brief quotations in critical articles, reviews, and pages where permission is specifically granted by the publisher.

STORIES FROM THE HEART
VOLUME 3

THIS BOOK IS A COMPILATION OF EVENTS
THAT TOOK PLACE THROUGHOUT MY LIFE.
SOME ARE STORIES ABOUT PEOPLE THAT I KNOW.
SOME ARE STORIES OF PEOPLE I MET ALONG THE WAY.
SOME OF THEM ARE TRUE EVENTS FROM MY OWN LIFE.
SOME ARE STORIES OF FOLKS I SAW ONLINE.

AS FOR THE LOVE STORIES....
THEY MIGHT BE TRUE.
OR
THEY MIGHT BE FICTITIOUS.

WHICH ONES ARE TRUE EVENTS?
THAT'S UP TO YOU TO FIGURE OUT.
I TRULY HOPE YOU ENJOY VOLUME THREE
AS MUCH AS YOU DID VOLUMES ONE AND TWO.

Tortured Soul With A Pen

Table of Contents

Dedication 1
Please Be Mine 2
Your Love Is
My Drug 6
Deeper Love 12
Love Me 14
What A Beautiful
Sight. 16
Your Heart 18
Your Beauty Within 20
Your Chocolate Lips 24
I More Than Like You ... 28
Hard Day. 32
Forever Isn't Enough ... 36
I Need You. 40
My Feelings For You 42
Two Languages 44
Trophy Husband 46
He Loved Me More 50
Hurt 52

BiPolar City 56
Michael 60
Michelle 64
Walter 68
Have You Ever? 72

I Got You Today
Mommy 76
I Just Know It 78
New Feet 80
Trapped In A Cage
Of Silence 84
His Speech is Frozen ... 88

Afraid Of Love 90
If You Could See 92
Love Is Love 94

Table of Contents

Perfect Angel 96
Sweet Pea. 100
My Baby Girl 104
I Love You Son 108
Please Come Back 112
Please Forgive Me 114
Wings 116
The Clock Is Ticking ... 118
Why Daddy Why? 122
Free From Your
Earthly Burdens 126
Thank You For The
Birthday Gift, Dad 130
Dale 134

Tidal Wave Of
Emotions 138
What? 142
Who Did This To Me ... 146
Racism 152
Equality 156
So Much
Destruction 158
I Want Us Back 162
If Heaven Had
Visiting Hours 166
Giving Flowers To
The Living 168
Uncle Bob Asked
For A Job 172
You Were Right 176
Fight or Flight 180

I Was Lost In
A Dream 184
Happily Ever
Without 186
Crash And Burn 188
Existence 190
The Night You
Promised To Stay 192
Loneliness Is
My Only Friend. 194
One Wish 196
If There Was
No Tomorrow 198
If I Never
Met You 200
Widow 202
Walking A New
Road Alone 204

I'm Outta My
Head Without You ... 208
My Grandma 214

Dedication

This book is dedicated to my grandma, like the rest of this series. She was my everything. She's in Heaven with my grandpa. She wasn't here to witness the birth of any of the books in this series, but I'm sending her a "Heavenly Edition" of Volume Three to add to Volumes One and Two.

My Pops joined my grandparents 20 months ago. My brother joined them last month. Volume Three is for all of you. We will all reunite one day.

Tortured Soul With A Pen

PLEASE BE MINE

PLEASE BE MINE,

NIGHT AFTER NIGHT.
WOMAN AFTER WOMAN.
I'M BORED.
BLONDES,
BRUNETTES,
EVERY COLOR AND NATIONALITY.

THEIR WALKS OF SHAME ARE BORING TO ME.

I WISH I WAS WITH YOU, AGAIN.
I MISS YOU.
I NEED YOU.
I LOVE YOU.

THEY ARE NOT LOVERS.
THEY'RE MERELY A DISTRACTION.
MY WAY OF PASSING TIME
GETTING PAST MY LONELINESS.

SOMETIMES THEY GIVE ME MONEY.
SOMETIMES THEY BUY ME THINGS.
SOMETIMES THEY JUST ADD TO MY BODY COUNT.

Tortured Soul With A Pen

I WISH I WAS WITH YOU, AGAIN.
I MISS YOU.
I NEED YOU.
I LOVE YOU.

WHEN WILL THIS ALL END?
WHEY WILL YOU BE MINE?
WHEN WILL I BE YOURS?
WHEN WILL YOU AND I BE ONE?

PLEASE BE MINE

Tortured Soul With A Pen

Your Love Is My Drug

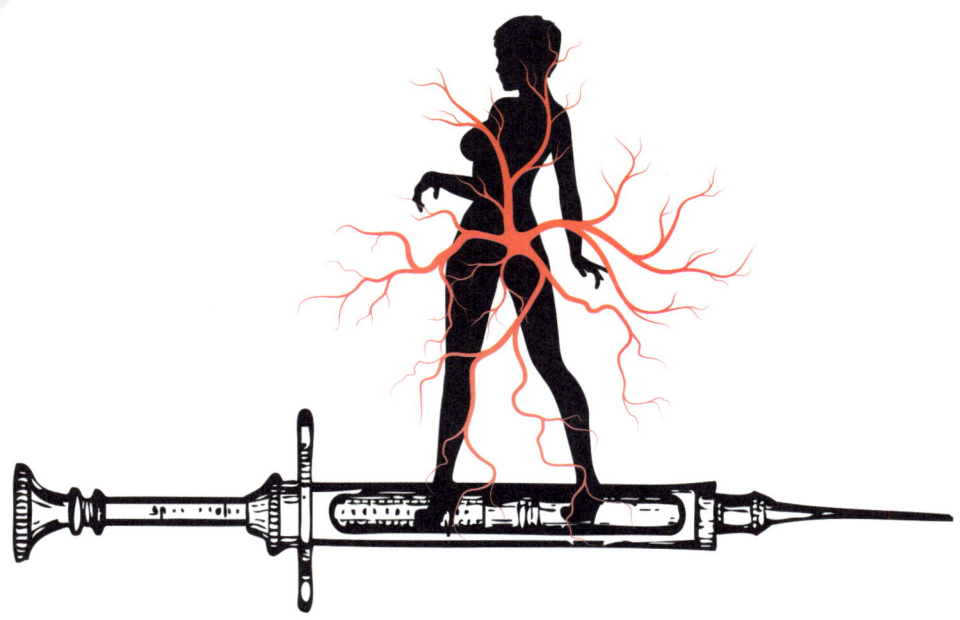

Your love enters my heart and soul.
Like a needle in my vein.

Better than heroin, X or cocaine.
I get so damn high.
I feel like I could fly.

Just talking to you gets me high.
But when we're apart is when I cry.
I love you so much.
When it comes to this, I'll never lie

I can't get enough of you like a drug.
And I'm happy to be addicted.

I'm so up and so down.
How am I so conflicted?

Do I need rehab?

Or a new girl?

She wouldn't be you.

I can't start something new.

I love you.

I need you.

I must've you.

Should I give up and walk away?

Should I dig deep and fight every day?

I'll fight if you'll fight too.

Since I need you & love you & must've you

I'll fight for us forever cause I know you will too

Your love enters my heart and soul like a needle in my vein.

Better than heroin, X or cocaine

As the poison or drugs enters my bloodstream

I feel an incredible turbulent,

high and yet at the same time a calming peace.

I know this high won't last long.
But I can get more when ever I want.
As with any drug.
I'm so happy to be addicted!
Are you a drug or are you medicine.
It's nearly impossible to tell.

Honestly I don't care either way.

At this point it's no longer a want. It's a need.
I need you. I need your needle to pierce my skin.
I need your poison to enter my vein.
I need your love to enter my soul.
I used to need this fix weekly or so.
Now it's turned into a daily habit.

I'm so up, I'm so down. Why am I so conflicted?
Soon, I'll need a constant IV of you.
Of your medicine. Of your poison.
I need your needle to get thru each day.
Soon, I'll need you for every function.

Will I survive this poison or will I overdose
and die from the very thing that made me feel
so alive in the first place.
Only time will tell.
As of right now I have the time.
At some point time will be based on the need
for the next fix.

Do I quit cold turkey and find a new girl,
a new fix, a new high?
If I do she won't be you, I'll never get that high.
Is it too late for me to even try?
Am I foolin myself? I know I'm an addict.
I know in my heart that I cannot quit.
I beg God to let me overdose,
for I cannot endure the painful withdrawals.

The absence of you in my veins,
in my bloodstream,
in my soul will destroy me.

I can't live thru the pain of being drug sick.
Sweating, shaking, begging and crying for one more fix.
Lord please allow me to die in my sleep
or awaken to never ending supply.
Of my poison
Of my medicine
Of my love
Of my dream come true.

I need you
I love you
I must've you

DEEPER LOVE

WHEN YOUR EYES SEE ME, THEY SEE....

A PRETTY FACE?

A SHAPELY BODY?

THANK YOU,

BUT YOU NEED TO ASK YOURSELF.....

WHAT DOES YOUR HEART SEE?

A LOVING WOMAN?

A WONDERFUL MOTHER?

WHAT DOES YOUR SOUL SEE?

AN HONEST AND FAITHFUL LOVER?

SOMEONE YOU CAN COUNT ON FOREVER?

IF YOU DON'T SEE ALL OF THESE,

YOUR LOVE FOR ME IS ONLY SKIN DEEP.

I NEED A DEEPER LOVE.

A SYNERGISTIC CONNECTION.

A SOULFUL LOVE.

A TRUE BOND.

I NEED TO BE ONE WITH YOU.

I NEED A DEEPER LOVE.

WOULD YOU PLEASE

HURRY UP

AND FALL IN LOVE WITH ME

ALREADY?

I WOKE UP SATURDAY MORNING
I LOOKED DOWN TO SEE THE TOP OF YOUR HEAD
LAYING ON MY CHEST
WHAT A BEAUTIFUL SIGHT.

YOUR SKIN ON MY SKIN.
BARE BREASTS ON MY RIBS.
YOUR FINGERTIPS CARESSING MY CHEST.
YOU MOANED AS I KISSED THE TOP OF YOUR HEAD.
I'M FALLING IN LOVE WITH YOU.

THE WARMTH OF OUR INTERLOCKED LEGS.
MY HAND NATURALLY CARESSED YOUR BACK
AS I LISTEN TO YOU ENJOY MY TOUCH.

THIS IS INTIMACY TIME.
TIME FOR OUR HEARTS TO LOVE EACH OTHER.
TIME FOR OUR SOULS TO BOND.
I'M FALLING IN LOVE WITH YOU.

YOU LOOKED UP AT ME.
AND WITHOUT A SOUND,
YOU PROFESSED YOUR LOVE FOR ME.
YOU SAID YOU WANT ME FOREVER
YOU'RE FALLING TOO.
WHAT A BEAUTIFUL SIGHT.

I'D BE HONORED IF YOU SAVE
A SPOT IN YOUR LOVING HEART FOR ME.
I KNOW IT IS A SPECIAL PLACE
FILLED WITH LOVE AND WARMTH.

I HAVE A BEAUTIFUL PLACE IN MY HEART
DESIGNED ESPECIALLY FOR YOU,
FULL OF LOVE, HONOR AND RESPECT.

WHEN I TELL YOU I LOVE YOU,
I'LL MEAN IT WITH ALL MY HEART & MY SOUL.
I DON'T USE THOSE WORDS OFTEN OR LIGHTLY.

I'M LOOKING FORWARD TO LOVING YOU....

Tortured Soul With A Pen

YOUR BEAUTY WITHIN

THERE'S SOMETHING ABOUT YOU
THAT I JUST CAN'T GET ENUF OF.....

IS IT YOUR SEDUCTIVE EYES?
OR YOUR SOFT, FULL LIPS?
OR YOUR BEAUTIFUL CHOCOLATE SKIN?

NO

IT'S YOUR BEAUTY WITHIN.

IS IT YOUR FULL, FIRM BREASTS?
OR YOUR STRONG, FLAT TUMMY?
OR YOUR PLUMP, ROUND REAR END?

NO

IT'S YOUR BEAUTY WITHIN.

IS IT THE WAY YOU KISS ME?
OR THE WAY YOU TOUCH ME?
OR IS IS IT YOUR LOVIN?

NO

IT'S YOUR BEAUTY WITHIN.

Tortured Soul With A Pen

Tortured Soul With A Pen

YOUR CHOCOLATE LIPS

SOME DAYS I JUST LOOK AT YOUR LIPS
AND THINK " HOW DID GOD CREATE SUCH A MASTERPIECE?
YOUR LIPS ARE SOFT, PLUMP AND FULL.
THE RASPBERRY CHOCOLATE COLORING IS GORGEOUS.

I WANT TO PUT MINE ON THEM
AND JUST KISS YOU ALL DAY
THEY'RE SUCH A BEAUTIFUL SIGHT
A TRUE WORK OF ART
BE PROUD OF THEIR BEAUTY

I HOLD YOUR FACE AND APPROACH SLOWLY
PARTIALLY FOR THE SENSUALITY OF GOING SLOWLY TO KISS YOU
IN PART SO I CAN SIMPLY TAKE IN THEIR VISUAL BEAUTY.
BEFORE I SPEND THE NEXT HOUR KISSING THEM.

I DRAW YOU BOTTOM LIP INTO MY MOUTH
I LICK IT
NIBBLE ON IT.
I RELEASE IT FROM MY MOUTH.

AND OUR TONGUES DANCE TOGETHER.
YOU PULL MY TONGUE INTO YOUR MOUTH
MY MIND INSTANTLY WANDERS.
YOU PULL BACK AND KISS MY LIPS.

HOW CAN YOUR CHOCOLATE LIPS
LOVE MY PINK ONES SO MUCH?

BUT THEY DO.

I PULL OUR LIPS APART TO STARE AGAIN
YOUR CHOCOLATE LIPS ARE A TRUE WORK OF ART.
I COULD LOOK AT THEM AND KISS THEM ALL DAY.
YOUR TONGUE LICKS MY LIPS.
"KISS ME AGAIN LOVER" YOU SAY.

I PLACE MY LIPS ON YOUR GORGEOUS CHOCOLATE LIPS.
BODY PARTS ARE HEATING UP,
SOME ARE GROWNG.

OUR HANDS WANDER.

CLOTHING REMOVED.

WE'LL BE MAKING LOVE SOON.

AND IT ALL STARTED WITH

YOUR CHOCOLATE LIPS.

I MORE THAN LIKE YOU

THERE'S AN OLD SAYING THAT GOES....
"LET ME COUNT THE WAYS I LOVE YOU."
WELL, I DON'T KNOW IF I LOVE YOU YET,
BUT I FEEL I'M WELL ON MY WAY.

I MORE THAN LIKE YOU

BUT THERE ARE CERTAIN THINGS I DO LOVE ABOUT YOU....

YOUR LAUGH

YOUR INTEGRITY

YOUR WIT

YOUR INTELLIGENCE

YOUR CHARM

YOUR SENSITIVITY

YOUR STRENGTH

YOUR MOTHERHOOD

YOU CARINGNESS

YOUR LOVINGNESS

YOUR RESPECT

YOUR VOCABULARY

YOUR FLATTERY TO ME

YOUR ACCEPTANCE OF MY FLATTERY AND CHARM

YOUR SELFLESSNESS

YOUR DESIRE TO TALK WITH ME

YOUR EFFORT TO FIT ME INTO YOUR BUSY LIFE

YOUR SMILE

YOUR GORGEOUS FACE

YOUR BEAUTIFUL BODY

YOUR SEX APPEAL

YOUR HEART

YOUR SOUL

YOU

I MORE THAN LIKE YOU

I'M LOOKING FORWARD TO SEE IF WE FALL IN LOVE.

THANK YOU FOR ALL YOU DO.

THANK YOU FOR BEING YOU.

THANK YOU, THAT'S IT, JUST THANK YOU.

Tortured Soul With A Pen

Tortured Soul With A Pen

HARD DAY

WELCOME HOME MY LOVE
YOU SAID YOU HAD A HARD DAY TODAY.
SO I LEFT WORK EARLY FOR YOU.
DINNER AND DESERT ARE ON THE WAY.

YOUR BATH TUB IS FILLING UP AS WE SPEAK.
COMPLETE WITH A BATH BOMB.
ALL OF YOUR BATHING PRODUCTS ARE THERE.
CANDLES ARE BURNING
R AND B MUSIC IS PLAYING.

THE BOOK YOU ARE READING IS AT THE TUB.
A GLASS OF CHAMPAGNE IS POURED.
A COUPLE OF FRESH BOTTLES ARE ON ICE WITHIN REACH.
STRAWBERRIES ARE THERE AS WELL.

GIVE ME YOUR PURSE, AND COAT.
GO GET UNDRESSED AND SOAK YOUR STRESSES AWAY.
I'LL BE HERE IN CASE YOU NEED ANYTHING
RING THE BELL THAT'S ON THE EDGE OF THE TUB
IF YOU NEED ANYTHING ELSE.

TOWELS AND YOUR ROBE ARE HANGING
BY THE TUB WHEN YOU'RE DONE.
TAKE YOUR TIME.
I'LL KEEP DINNER WARM.
AFTER WE EAT, I'LL GIVE YOU A SENSUAL, DEEP TISSUE MASSAGE.

THE REST OF THE NIGHT IS UP TO YOU.....
MOVIE OF YOUR CHOICE?
MUSIC AND CANDLES?
CONVERSATION BY THE FIREPLACE?

IT'S YOUR NIGHT MY LOVE.
ENJOY IT.

Tortured Soul With A Pen

Tortured Soul With A Pen

FOREVER ISN'T ENOUGH

FOREVER ISN'T ENOUGH

AT FIRST THAT MAY SOUND GREEDY,
SINCE NO LOVERS GET FOREVER.
BUT SINCE WE JUST MET,
I CAN'T HELP BUT FEEL SLIGHTED.

I REPEAT MY FEELINGS....
FOREVER ISN'T ENOUGH

ALL THE LOVERS I KNOW
HAVE A PAST
SOME ARE YEARS
OTHERS ARE DECADES

THEY'RE ALREADY LIVING AND LOVING
IN THEIR FOREVER

TODAY IS OUR FIRST DAY AS LOVERS.
SO WE DON'T HAVE A PAST.
A PAST OF LOVING NIGHTS.
VACATIONS, HOUSES, KIDS, PETS

I REPEAT MY FEELINGS....
FOREVER ISN'T ENOUGH

I NEED MORE TIME
LOVING YOU, CARING FOR YOU,
BEING WITH YOU. BONDING WITH YOU
BECOMING ONE WITH YOU

MORE TIME BUILDING MEMORIES
MORE TIME LAUGHING
MORE TIME PLANNING OUR FOREVER.
EVEN THOUGH....

FOREVER ISN'T ENOUGH

Tortured Soul With A Pen

I Need You

It's a lazy Sunday morning.

I have nothing to do.

All the cleaning and chores are done.

I wanna spend the day with you,

But I can't.

Instead, I'll spend the day thinking about you.

Chatting with you.

I've said it before,

I'll take you any way I can get you.

There's miles and miles between us.

I'm working on fixing this.

I'm on my grind every day

Looking for work and a home near you.

I'm very close to making it happen.

Sometimes I close my eyes

And I see you right in front of me.

I see us enjoying the day together.

Until we can be together physically.

I'd love to be together spiritually.

In many ways, this will build a stronger foundation.

Tortured Soul With A Pen

MY FEELINGS FOR YOU

BEING WITH YOU WARMS MY SOUL.
YOU MAKE MY HEART SMILE.
THE BUTTERFLIES YOU GIVE MY TUMMY
NEVER SLOW DOWN THEIR MOVEMENT

IT'S NATURAL FOR ME TO CHARM YOU.
TO FLATTER YOU FREQUENTLY.
TO PUT YOU FIRST IS ALL I KNOW.

YOU SAID THIS SCARES YOU A BIT.

I CAN SLOW IT DOWN.
I CAN PUMP MY BRAKES A LIL BIT.
BUT JUST KNOW THESE FEELINGS ARE HERE.

IN CASE YOU MISS THEM.
I CAN RELEASE THEM AGAIN.
THEY'RE HERE,
JUST FOR YOU.

Tortured Soul With A Pen

TWO LANGUAGES

WE SPEAK DIFFERENT LANGUAGES.
BUT AS THE SAYING GOES
THE LANGUAGE OF LOVE IS UNIVERSAL.

AS I LOOK INTO YOUR EYES
A SMILE CONSUMES YOUR FACE.
IT MATCHES THE ONE ON MINE.

YOU WARM MY HEART
YOU WARM MY SOUL
AND IT SHOWS IN THE WAY I LOOK AT YOU

SO MY WORDS GET LOST IN TRANSLATION
WATCH HOW I LOOK AT YOU
IT SAYS EVERYTHING MY VOICE CAN'T

Tortured Soul With A Pen

TROPHY HUSBAND

I HAVE HER HEART.

I HAVE HER SOUL.

I HAVE HER SEXUALLY...

WHENEVER I WANT

I PLEASURE HER OVER AND OVER AGAIN.

I BRING HER ECSTASY.

I'M HER SOURCE OF SEXUAL AND SENSUAL ECSTASY

I'M HER SOURCE OF PLEASURE.

ORGASM AFTER ORGASM.

I MAKE HER FACE NUMB.

YOU DON'T HAVE HER HEART.

YOU DON'T HAVE HER SOUL.

YOU DON'T HAVE HER BODY.

YOU DON'T HAVE HER RESPECT.

WHAT DO YOU REALLY HAVE?

SOMEONE TO SHARE AN OCCASIONAL MEAL WITH?

WHEN SHE'S NOT OUT "SHOPPING"?

THAT'S WHEN SHE'S WITH ME!

IF I TOLD YOU ALL THIS.....

YOU'D CRUMBLE AND DIE.

YOU SAY, "I SAVED YOU FROM HIM."

SAVED HER FROM WHAT?

A LIFE OF.....

FUN?

LAUGHTER ?

PLEASEURE?

SEXUALITY ?

SENSUALITY?

PASSION?

DON'T GET IT TWISTED.

YOUR KIDS ARE WHAT KEEP HER THERE.

NOT YOU....

TROPHY HUSBAND.

Tortured Soul With A Pen

Tortured Soul With A Pen

HE LOVED ME MORE

IT WAS NEVER A MATTER OF
WHO I LOVED MORE
HIM OR YOU?

THAT'S AN EASY ONE TO ANSWER
YOU WERE MY EVERYTHING
MY MAGIC MAN

BUT YOU WERE MAGIC TO A LOT OF GIRLS
I COULDN'T SHARE YOU
THAT'S WHY I LEFT YOU
YOU KNOW THIS

I CHOSE HIM
HE LOVED ME MORE
HE LOVED ME FAIR

I MISS YOU
YOU LOVED ME WILD, SEXY, CRAZY!
GOD I MISS YOU!
YOUR CRAZY, SEXY "LET'S DO IT ANYWHERE ATTITUDE"
IS INTOXICATING
WANNA GO DO IT IN THE PARK?
I HAVE BLANKETS IN THE CAR

Tortured Soul With A Pen

Hurt

I'M SCARED,

SO SCARED

I LOVED YOU YEARS AGO

WE FOUND EACH OTHER AGAIN

OUR LOVE BLOSSOMED AGAIN SO QUICKLY

I LOVE YOU

I LUST FOR YOU

I MISS YOU

SO MUCH IT HONESTLY HURTS

MY HEAD IS AT WAR WITH MY HEART

I DON'T WANT TO HURT ANYONE.

NOT HIM.

NOT YOU.

NOT ME.

BUT ULTIMATELY SOMEONE WILL HURT.

FOR SURE, I WILL.

WHO ELSE DO I HURT?

A MAN THAT HAS NEVER HURT ME?
OR A MAN THAT CRUSHED ME AS A TEENAGER,
WHO IS ALSO MY DREAM COME TRUE

HOW DID WE LET THIS HAPPEN?
ARE WE DESTINED FOR EACH OTHER,
WITH A HUGE DETOUR?
OR IS IT OUR FATE TO HURT EACH OTHER?

Tortured Soul With A Pen

Tortured Soul With A Pen

BIPOLAR CITY

BIPOLAR CITY

YOU SQUEEZED US OUT OF SURROUNDING CITIES
INTO A LAND NAMED AFTER AN OAK TREE.
THE NEIGHBORHOODS QUICKLY GREW ROUGH FROM CONGESTION.
BUILDINGS NOT BEING MAINTAINED
INFRASTRUCTURE ABANDONED US
WE DID THE BEST WITH WHAT WE HAD.

FOR YEARS, YOU IGNORED US AND OUR CITY
LANDLORDS/SLUMLORDS MISTREATED US
YOU JUDGED US AND CONVICTED US

NOW YOU'RE MOVING BACK
SQUEEZING US OUT AGAIN
BLEACHING OUR CULTURE AWAY.
GENTRIFICATION YOU CALL IT.

WE CALL IT A HOSTILE TAKE OVER!
BUYING UP BUILDINGS FOR PENNIES ON THE DOLLAR.
PUSHING OUT OUR BUISINESSES.
BUYING AND RESTORING HOMES FOR EVEN LESS.

EVICTING TENANTS!
MOVE OUT YOU SAY.

HERE'S A DOLLAR!
"YOU SHOULD BE HAPPY. YOU MADE A NICKEL".
WE'RE NOT GRATEFUL, WE DIDN'T ASK FOR ANY OF THIS.

YOU SEGREGATED US.
WE DEALT WITH IT!
NOW YOU WANNA INTEGRATE US,
ONLY SOME OF US.

YOU WANT TO INTEGRATE US YOUR WAY!
YOUR WAY IS NOT OUR WAY!
YOUR WAY IS NOT FAIR OR EQUITABLE!
YOUR WAY IS COLOR DRIVEN!
YOUR WAY IS WRONG!!

EASE YOUR MINDS BY SAYING YOUR BETTERING OUR CITY?
RAISING THE VALUE OF EVERYTHING?
YOU'RE INVADING US!
WE DON'T WANT YOU HERE!
WE DON'T NEED YOU HERE!
WE NEED INFRASTRUCTURE WITHOUT STRINGS ATTACHED!
WE NEED A CITY THAT WE CAN STILL AFFORD TO LIVE IN!

OUR CITY MAY NOT BE PERFECT
OUR CITY MAY NOT BE TO YOUR LIKING
YOU'RE DOING THIS BECAUSE THE CITY BY THE BAY
IS TOO EXPENSIVE AND OVER CROWDED

SO YOU DECIDED THAT THIS WILL BE YOUR NEW CITY!!

WRONG,
THIS IS OUR CITY!!
OUR OAKLAND
KINDLY LEAVE
LET US BE.

Tortured Soul With A Pen

MICHAEL

MY FRIEND CAME BY TODAY.
HE TOOK ME TO THE BARBER SHOP
GOT ME A SHAVE AND LINED ME UP
I DON'T LOOK HOMELESS ANYMORE

BUT I AM

THE FOLKS IN THE SHOP
LOADED ME UP WITH BAGS AND BAGS
FROM THE GROCERY STORE
FOOD AND SUPPLIES FOR WEEKS, MAYBE LONGER

MY FRIEND HAD MY PICTURE
UP ON THE BILLBOARD
IN TIME SQUARE
LOCAL CELEBRITY FOR TODAY

A FUND RAISER?
PERFECT STRANGERS
PERFECT ANGELS.
GO FUND ME
$44,000

I CAN GET A NEW WHEELCHAIR
AN APARTMENT WITH A BED
CLOTHES & SHOWERS

DIGNITY & PEACE

I LOVE MY FRIEND
I LOVE THOSE STRANGERS
I LOVE GO FUND ME

I LOVE THE LORD
I LOVE MY LIFE

Tortured Soul With A Pen

Tortured Soul With A Pen

MICHELLE

I TOOK AN OATH TO PROTECT AND SERVE.
SO OFTEN WE FORGET THAT PART OF OUR JOBS.
WHEN WE'RE CHASING BAD GUYS
AND ARRESTING CRIMINALS

I CAME ACROSS A WOMAN I HADN'T SEEN BEFORE.
SHE LOOKED HOMELESS AND DOWN.
I ASKED HER WHAT HER NAME WAS.
MICHELLE, SHE SAID WITH A SHAMEFUL LOOK.

HER CLOTHES WERE TATTERED AND DIRTY.
HER T-SHIRT HAD A MESSAGE WRITTEN IN MARKER.
HOMELESS: THE FASTEST WAY OF BECOMING NOBODY.

SHE SAW ME LOOK AT THE MESSAGE.
SHE BOWED HER HEAD AND CONFIRMED IT.
SHE'S BEEN ON THE STREETS FOR A FEW YEARS.
SHE LOST HER JOB AND HOME, THE REST IS HISTORY.

I ASKED HER IF SHE WAS HUNGRY.
SHE NODDED YES. SHE HADN'T EATEN IN DAYS.
I PULLED UP SOME WOODEN BLOCKS TO SIT ON.
I RETURNED WITH A FEW PIZZAS AND DRINKS.

SHE SAID THANK YOU AND GOD BLESS YOU.
I RETURNED THE BLESSING WITH A PRAYER FOR HER.
WE ATE AND TALKED FOR AN HOUR OR SO.
I LEARNED A LOT ABOUT MICHELLE THAT DAY.

SHE HAD A GOOD JOB AND HOME TILL SHE LOST THEM.
SHE IS A KIND AND LOVING PERSON.
SHE LOVED HER DOG TILL SHE HAD TO GIVE HIM AWAY.

SHE DOES NOT DO DRUGS OR ALCOHOL.
SHE'S NOT BITTER TOWARDS PEOPLE WHO JUDGE HER.
SHE STILL HAS AN UNBREAKABLE BOND WITH GOD.

MICHELLE & I CAME UP WITH A PLAN FOR HER FUTURE.
BABY STEPS, BUT FORWARD MOTION NONE THE LESS.
CHURCH AT LEAST TWICE A WEEK.

REGULAR STAYS AT THE SHELTER DURING THE WEEK.
SHE'LL STAY WITH ME & MY WIFE ON THE WEEKENDS.
AND MORE GOOD TALKS LIKE THE ONE WE HAD TODAY.
I'M GONNA TAKE HER SHOPPING WEEKLY.

AND WHEN SHE'S READY, I'LL GET HER A JOB INTERVIEW.
SOMETIMES PEOPLE JUST NEED AN EXTENDED HAND.
WE SHOULD ALL HELP ONE ANOTHER.
IT'S VERY REWARDING.

NEVER LOOK DOWN ON SOMEONE UNLESS YOU'RE HELPING THEM UP.
TO PROTECT AND SERVE.
THIS SHOULD BE EVERYONE'S MANTRA.

THANK YOU MICHELLE.

Tortured Soul With A Pen

WALTER

I MET A MAN TODAY THAT STUCK IN MY HEAD.
MOST PEOPLE FORGET HIM IMMEDIATELY.
HIS NAME IS WALTER.

WALTER WAS WALKING ALONG AN OVERPASS IN MY TOWN.
HE WAS DISHEVELED AND LOOKED HOMELESS.
HE WAS WALKING SLOWLY.
LOOKING FOR ANYTHING OF VALUE ON THE GROUND.

STRANGELY ENOUGH
I HAD 1 "BLESSING BAG" LEFT.
"BLESSING BAGS" ARE JUST THAT...

BAGS I MADE UP FOR HOMELESS PEOPLE.
THEY HAVE SUPPLIES, SNACKS, WIPES, WATER ETC.
I HANDED HIM HIS BAG AND $10

HE THANKED ME AN ASKED ME MY NAME.
WE CHATTED AS WE WALKED BACK TOWARDS MY CAR.
HE SAID HE NEVER THOUGHT HE'D BE HOMELESS.
HE'S 65, BUT LOOKS EVERY BIT OF 75.

HE DIDN'T ELABORATE ON HIS SITUATION.
HIS ONLY FOCUS WAS GETTING TO CLEVELAND.
HIS NEPHEW MARK WAS THERE.
WALTER SAID MARK IS THE BEST MAN HE KNOWS.

MARK JUST CONTACTED COVID
HE ALREADY SUFFERS FROM A NEURO MUSCULAR DISEASE.
HE'S NOT DOING WELL.

HE'S VERY SYMPTOMATIC.

WE PARTED WAYS AFTER OUR CHAT
I WISHED HIM WELL
HE SAID "GOD BLESS YOU"

PLEASE KEEP MARK AND WALTER IN YOUR PRAYERS.
AND ALL HOMELESS PEOPLE.
THEY'RE JUST PEOPLE HAVING A HARDER TIME THAN YOU ARE.

PS...THIS IS A TRUE STORY. IT JUST HAPPENED TEN MINUTES AGO.

Tortured Soul With A Pen

HAVE YOU EVER?

HAVE YOU EVER PULLED OUT A DIRTY PAIR OF JEANS
FROM THE GARBAGE DUMPSTER AND PUT THEM ON.
ONLY TO BE HAPPY BECAUSE THEY WERE CLEANER
THAN ONES YOU HAD ON.
HAVE YOU EVER EATEN A PART OF A SANDWICH THAT YOU FOUND
ON THE GROUND
EVEN THOUGH YOU KNOW IT'S DISGUSTING
BECAUSE IT'S THE ONLY FOOD YOU MAY GET ALL DAY.

HAVE YOU EVER PANHANDLED FOR MONEY?
IN ALL IT'S SHAME?
KNOWING THAT YOU'LL PROBABLY JUST SPEND THE MONEY ON
ALCOHOL
EVEN THOUGH YOU KNOW IF YOU SAVED IT
YOU COULD PROBABLY CHANGE YOUR LIFESTYLE.
IT JUST SEEMS LIKE SAVING IT WOULD TAKE TOO LONG.
SO GETTING DRUNK AND NUMB SEEMS TO BE THE QUICK FIX.

HAVE YOU EVER HAD TO SLEEP WITH ALL OF YOUR BELONGINGS
SAFELY TUCKED UNDER YOUR HEAD AND IN YOUR ARMS?
MEAGER AS THEY MAY BE
THEY'RE ALL YOU HAVE.
HOPING NO ONE ROBS YOU IN THE NIGHT AS YOU TRY TO SLEEP
ON A PARK BENCH, ON THE GRASS UNDER A TREE OR WORSE....
THE CONCRETE?

HAVE YOU EVER HAD TO ASK A TEENAGER TO USE THE BATHROOM
AT A FAST FOOD JOINT
SO YOU COULD ATTEMPT TO WASH UP AND PUT THE SAME FILTHY
CLOTHES BACK ON
WITH SHAME ON YOUR FACE AND A SHATTERED HEART?
ONLY TO HEAR HIM LAUGH WITH HIS CO-WORKERS
AS HE SAYS "NO, GET OUTTA HERE YOU BUM".

HAVE YOU EVER CRIED YOURSELF TO SLEEP UNDER A TREE IN THE
HOT SUN WITH NO WATER
BECAUSE YOU WERE TOO AFRAID TO SLEEP AT NIGHT?
HOLDING A PICTURE OF THE FAMILY THAT YOU USED TO HAVE.
BEFORE YOU LOST YOUR JOB YEARS AGO.

HAVE YOU EVER CRIED AS YOU SAW A BEAUTIFUL WOMAN
PLAYING WITH HER KIDS IN THE PARK?
KNOWING THAT THEY DIDN'T EVEN RECOGNIZE YOU
YOUR HAIR AND BEARD LONG
DREADLOCKED FROM YEARS OF GROWTH AND NEGLECT?
AND YOU JUST WANNA GO BACK HOME WITH THEM
AND BE A FAMILY AGAIN.

PLEASE THINK OF THESE PEOPLE WHEN YOU SAY " I DON'T HAVE ANY CASH". A COUPLE DOLLARS TO YOU COULD MAKE A HUGE DIFFERENCE IN THEIR LIVES. ALSO, PLEASE DON'T JUDGE THEM.... HELP THEM, INSTEAD.

Tortured Soul With A Pen

I GOT YOU TODAY,

MOMMY

I LEARNED MANY THINGS FROM YOU.
ONE OF MY FAVORITE THINGS I LEARNED
IS HOW TO BE STRONG.

I LEARNED BY WATCHING YOU.
YOU ALWAYS HAVE IT ALL TOGETHER.
YOU'RE SO STRONG.
YOU'RE NOT AFRAID OF ANYTHING OR ANYONE.

YOU PROTECT US.
YOU CARE FOR US.
YOU LOVE US.

YOU HOLD US DOWN ALL YEAR LONG.
PLEASE MOMMY, TAKE A DAY OFF?
I GOT YOU TODAY, MOMMY.
COME LAY YOUR HEAD ON MY CHEST.
CLOSE YOUR EYES AND REST.
JUST BE, MOMMY, JUST BE.....

I GOT YOU TODAY, MOMMY,
I GOT YOU.

Tortured Soul With A Pen

I JUST KNOW IT

IT'S OK MOMMY
PLEASE DON'T CRY
LET ME WIPE YOUR TEARS

HE'LL COME HOME
MAYBE TONIGHT
MAYBE TOMORROW
I JUST KNOW IT

HE WON'T BE GONE FOREVER
DADDY WILL COME HOME ONE DAY
I JUST KNOW IT

Tortured Soul With A Pen

NEW FEET

My baby girl got new feet today.
Yes, you heard that right.
She was born with no legs
From the knees down.

You would think she'd be sad.
But she was ecstatic.
Like it was Christmas morning.
I guess for her.... this was even better.

She was giggling and laughing.
I asked "are you getting new feet"?
She repeated her answer over and over
"Yes, yes, yes".
That's all she kept saying,
Thru all the giggles

I don't know if I've ever seen her happier.
I was conflicted inside
I wouldn't let her see that
She's a little empath, herself

She'd want to know why I was crying
Then she would try to fix it
She is too young to understand
She's only 3

I turned away as I was filming
I needed a private moment
I wiped the salty tears from my cheeks
Just before she saw me

She's so amazing
I learned from her today
I was so sad for my baby
But I learned that if she's not sad....
Maybe I shouldn't be sad

She's so happy
That made me happy
I'll cry more when I'm alone, tonight

Right now, I'll share in her delight
It's beautiful to watch her
You'd think she was getting a new toy
Or perhaps a puppy

God sure works his magic
Right when I need it.

Thank you Lord
Thank you
For my baby's New Feet

Tortured Soul With A Pen

TRAPPED IN A CAGE OF SILENCE

I TRY TO COMMUNICATE WITH YOU
IT JUST DOESN'T SEEM TO WORK FOR ME

I TRY AND I TRY
I FAIL AND I FAIL
THANK YOU FOR BEING PATIENT

I FEEL TRAPPED IN MY CAGE OF SILENCE

THANK YOU FOR TRYING ALTERNATIVE METHODS
SOME OF US DON'T GET THOSE OPTIONS.
SOME OF US ARE ABLE TO WRITE ON PAPER,
WHILE SOME CAN ONLY POINT.
SOME CAN TRY TO SPEAK,
WHILE OTHERS CANNOT SPEAK AT ALL.

JUST SO EVERYONE IS CLEAR....WE'RE NOT STUPID
WE'RE ACTUALLY CLOSER TO GENIUS,
THAN WE ARE TO MENTALLY CHALLENGED
THANK YOU FOR NOT TEASING ME.
SOME OF US ARE NOT AS LUCKY.

WE FEEL TRAPPED IN OUR CAGE OF SILENCE

WE ARE OBSERVERS AT TIMES.
WE ARE GENTLE AND LOVING.
WE ARE PEACE SEEKING.
AT TIMES WE DO GET FRUSTRATED.

WE ARE ALWAYS DRIVEN BY LOVE.
IN THIS ASPECT, WE ARE REALLY
MORE ADVANCED THAN YOU.
MAYBE WE HAVE THE ADVANTAGE
WHEN IT REALLY MATTERS....WE ONLY SEE LOVE

WE ARE TRAPPED IN OUR CAGE OF SILENCE.

IF WE OBSESS OVER A NARROW RANGE OF INTERESTS.
IF WE REPEAT THE SAME BEHAVIOR FREQUENTLY.
OR IF WE GET FRUSTRATED OVER MINOR CHANGES.
PLEASE UNDERSTAND WE STRUGGLE SOMETIMES.

AGAIN, WE'RE NOT STUPID.
WE JUST LEARN AND COMMUNICATE DIFFERENTLY.
WE NEED YOUR HELP WITH CERTAIN THINGS.
WE WILL HELP YOU TO TRULY UNDERSTAND LOVE.

WE REALLY ARE TRAPPED IN OUR CAGE OF SILENCE.
PLEASE HELP UNLOCK THIS CAGE.

HIS SPEECH IS FROZEN

HE IS MY SON AND I LOVE HIM INFINITY.
HE IS ON THE SPECRUM.
HIS SPEECH IS FROZEN.

HE MAY NEVER BE VERBAL
BUT WE COMMUNICATE....
OUR WAY.....
THRU LOVE.

AFRAID OF LOVE

WHY ARE SO MANY AFRAID OF LOVE?

LOVE IS A BASIC HUMAN NEED.

LOVE MAKES US FEEL WANTED AND DESIRED.

IT MAKES US FEEL GOOD INSIDE.

LOVE IS THE GREATEST EMOTION OF ALL!

LOVE CAN GET YOU THRU THE HARDEST OF DAYS.

AND THE HARDEST OF TIMES.

SOMETIMES IT'S THE ONE THING THAT GETS US UP IN THE MORNING.

ALL YOU NEED IS LOVE, RIGHT?

LOVE CONQUERS ALL!

LOVE IS BLIND,

PUPPY LOVE,

A MOTHER'S LOVE,

LOVE AT FIRST SIGHT....

THEY ALL CAN'T BE WRONG.

RUN TOWARDS LOVE,

NOT AWAY FROM IT.

LOVE IS NOT TO BE FEARED,

BUT REVERED.

LOVE IS THE GREATEST EMOTION OF ALL!

If You Could See

IF YOU COULD SEE THE SCARS
THAT MENTAL ABUSE CAUSES,

I'D BE DISFIGURED FOR LIFE.
FORTUNATELY, I HIDE THEM WELL.
OTHERWISE, NO ONE WOULD TALK TO ME.

love is love

LOVE
IT DOES CHANGE AND MORPH
IT EVOLVES OVER TIME
BUT THE PURITY OF IT REMAINS

LOVE IS BEAUTIFUL
LOVE IS OUR BEST EMOTION
IT'S THE ONLY EMOTION THAT
CAN TAKE YOU TO THE VERY TOP
THEN DROP YOU OFF AT THE VERY,
VERY BOTTOM

LOVE IS LOVE

Perfect Angel

PERFECT ANGEL,

I'M SO GLAD TO FINALLY MEET YOU.

YOU ARRIVED EARLY.

UNFORTUNATELY TOO EARLY..

MY SOUL IS SHATTERED.

AND MY HEART IS BROKEN.

BECAUSE I HAVE TO SAY GOODBYE TO YOU...

ON THE VERY DAY WE MET.

BUT MY HEART WAS BLESSED WITH YOUR ARRIVAL.

AND I'LL BE FOREVER THANKFUL.

MY SPIRIT WILL BE FOREVER BETTER.

AFTER HOLDING YOU IN THE HOSPITAL..

AND MY SOUL WILL BE FOREVER CHANGED

AFTER CREATING AN ABSOLUTELY

PERFECT ANGEL

I HAD SO MANY INCREDIBLE PLANS

FOR YOU

FOR US

BUT THEY WILL WAIT IN MY HEART

UNTIL WE MEET AGAIN.

You're going to Heaven today.
Mommy will be there in the future..
Once I'm there, nothing will separate us again.

For now we can talk to each other
Thru prayer and signs
The other angels will teach you how.
I will miss you each and every day.

I will think of you always.
I await out reunion.
Until then, you will always be...
My Perfect Angel

Tortured Soul With A Pen

Sweet Pea

As we look down at you.

Our eyes leak rivers onto our cheeks.

You're our daughter.

Whom we love and have protected over the years.

We couldn't stop this day from arriving.

But the surgeon has the skills to be successful.

Jesus is watching over you.

We earned these wings for days like this.

He is watching over you because we love you

As does he.

He will not allow the surgeons to fail.

Mom watched over us for each of our round ones.

And she was successful.

My Cancer returned

Mom needed me to help you thru today

Jesus called for me.

I came willingly

Go to sleep while the surgeons do God's work.

When you awaken.

You'll be rid of this ugly tumor...forever.

You'll have to rest for weeks

Your remission will be an uphill battle

You can do this.

We've brought an old friend back

To help you thru your recovery.

He loves you immensely.

It will be your choice if you'd like him to stay

Or go after you're in remission.

He wants to be with you forever.

But he will walk away, if that is you wish.

He'll be ready if you ever need to call on him again.

No matter the reason. A & F (Always and Forever)

Now close your eyes.

Jesus has blessed the surgeons hands.

You'll need to rest a lot these next several weeks.

Call on your Superman when you need him.

He'll be there.

He promised us.

The medicine enters your veins.

Rest. the doctors will fix your body.

Jesus. mom and I will watch over you

Your Superman is there too

We love you Sweet Pea.

You'll be better when you awaken.

We promise.

Love mom and dad.

Tortured Soul With A Pen

MY BABY GIRL

SHE DIED ON THE SCENE.
I KEPT HER IN ICU FOR 15 DAYS
I COULDN'T LET HER GO
OUR PRIEST, MY HUSBAND AND THE HOSPITAL
FINALLY MADE ME

A HIT-AND-RUN DRIVER
ON HER 1ST DAY OF SCHOOL
MY HUSBAND AND I PRACTICED FOR A WHOLE WEEK
SHE KNEW EXACTLY HOW TO GET TO SCHOOL SAFELY.
THIS WAS THE 1ST TIME WE LET HER GO ANYWHERE ALONE
AND NOW SHE'S GONE.

THE DRIVER SAID THEY WERE DRIVING THE SPEED LIMIT.
THIS IS IMPOSSIBLE
SHE BROKE BOTH MY DAUGHTER'S FEMURS
SNAPPED HER NECK.
BROKE EVERY BONE IN HER FACE.
KNOCKED OUT EVERY SINGLE TOOTH IN HER MOUTH.
HER EYES ALMOST CAME OUT OF HER FACE

MY DAUGHTER WAS A GOOD KID.

SHE DIDN'T DESERVE THIS.
SHE SHOULD BE WITH US RIGHT NOW.
SHE LEFT OUR HOME AT 6:53.
BY 7:00 SHE WAS DEAD.
SHE ONLY HAD 9 BIRTHDAYS
I WANT MORE
I CAN NEVER HOLD HER AGAIN.
NEVER
I NEED HER IN MY ARMS
SHE WAS AN ONLY CHILD

NO TIRE MARKS ON THE STREET
THE DRIVER WENT TO THE GAS STATION
FILLED UP HER CAR
CALLED THE TOW TRUCK
CALLED HER MOM FOR A RIDE
AND WENT TO WORK
LIKE IT WAS A REGULAR DAY
ABSOLUTELY NO CARE IN THE WORLD.

Tortured Soul With A Pen

Tortured Soul With A Pen

I
LOVE
YOU
SON

I BOUGHT A COFFIN TODAY.
IT WAS ONLY 3 1/2 FEET LONG.
WHY SO SMALL YOU ASK?
CAUSE THAT AS BIG AS MY SON NEEDS.

HE WAS 6 YEARS OLD.
THE SUN ROSE YESTERDAY WITH HIM NOT HERE.
HE BATTLED A VERY RARE DISEASE FOR 4 YEARS.
HE FOUGHT LIKE A CHAMP TILL THE END.

HIS IMMUNE SYSTEM JUST ERODED.
NEAR THE END HE COULDN'T TALK, SEE OR EVEN BLINK.
TO SAY MY HEART IS DESTROYED IS AN UNDERSTATEMENT.
I'LL NEVER BE THE SAME.

I HAD 6 FATHER'S DAYS WITH HIM.
I WANT MORE!
I DESERVE MORE!
I NEED MORE!

SEVENTEEN DOCTORS,
OVER 100 APPOINTMENTS,
COULDN'T SAVE HIM.
NO ONE COULD.

PLEASE DO MY SON AND I A FEW FAVORS_

SQUEEZE YOUR KIDS EXTRA TIGHT.
TELL THEM YOU LOVE THEM OFTEN.
MAKE SURE THEY REALLY HEAR YOU.
BE PATIENT WITH THEM.
MESSES CAN BE CLEANED UP.
ACCIDENTS CAN BE REPAIRED.

PLEASE FEEL BLESSED THAT THEY'RE HEALTHY.
IF THEY HAVE A SPECIAL TALENT, PUSH THEM.
IF THEY REQUIRE MORE ATTENTION, HELP THEM.

JUST LOVE THEM EXTRA.
AS I CAN'T ANYMORE.

I LOVE YOU SON.

Tortured Soul With A Pen

Tortured Soul With A Pen

PLEASE COME BACK

I'M SO NUMB.

I DON'T KNOW HOW TO DO THIS WITHOUT YOU.

I HAVE A VIDEO OF THE LAST TIME I SAW YOU.

I WATCH IT SO MUCH,

I'M AFRAID I'LL WEAR IT OUT

SON, I NEED YOU HERE

I MISS YOU MORE THAN ANYONE COULD IMAGE.

THE PAIN OF LOSING A SON

THIS HURTS DEEP INTO MY SOUL

THE PAIN IS MORE INTENSE THAN I EVER IMAGINED.

Please Forgive Me 2

I took a man's life today.

It was premeditated and planned.

I am extremely sorry Lord.

Please Forgive Me.

He hurt my family.

And took them away.

That shattered my heart.

I was out of my head at the time..

I tried to forgive him.

I failed.

I was in too much pain.

Please Forgive Me.

Please Forgive Me.

Tortured Soul With A Pen

WINGS

ISN'T IT BEAUTIFUL WHEN
YOU WATCH AN ANGEL EARN THEIR WINGS
RIGHT IN FRONT OF YOUR EYES
RIGHT HERE ON EARTH

The Clock Is Ticking

I FEEL THE END IS SOON
IT'S JUST A MATTER OF TIME.
HOW MUCH TIME?

NO ONE KNOWS
BUT I KNOW IT'S NOT LONG
YOU'RE IN A NEW PLACE NOW

I FEEL LIKE THE CLOCK IS TICKING

YOU WERE ALWAYS SO STRONG
A TRUE LEADER
KING OF YOUR CASTLE

THANKFULLY, YOU'RE NOT IN PAIN
YOUR BODY IS GIVING UP
YOU'RE A FRACTION OF YOURSELF

I FEEL LIKE THE CLOCK IS TICKING

I WANT YOU HERE FOREVER
THAT'S SELFISH, I KNOW
I NEED TO LET YOU GO

BUT HOW?

I'm not ready
I'll never be ready

I know this

You do need to go
When you're ready
It's not up to me

I know the clock is ticking

Tortured Soul With A Pen

Tortured Soul With A Pen

Why Daddy, Why?

ALLS I WANTED YOU TO DO WAS LOVE ME!

AS I SCREAMED.....
"WHY DADDY WHY?
"WHY CAN'T YOU LOVE ME"!!

THAT'S ALL I WANTED.
"WHY DADDY WHY"?

TO THE TOP OF MY VOICE
I SCREAMED....
"WHY DADDY WHY"?

I POUNDED ON HIS CHEST.
AS HE LAY THERE IN HIS CASKET
I FELL TO THE FLOOR SOBBING.
MOMMY AND SISSY PICKED ME UP OFF THE FLOOR.

"I'M OK MOMMY"
"I'M OK SISSY."
"I'M OK."
"I'M GOOD"
I SAID TO ALL

THIS WAS THE BEGINNING OF SOMETHING.
OF A NEW CHAPTER.
I WAS A MOTHER FOR A FEW YEARS BY THEN

THIS WAS A NEW DAY.
I BECAME A NEW ME THAT DAY.
I'LL STAND ON MY OWN, ALONE.
WITH THE ONE I CAN RELY ON……ME.

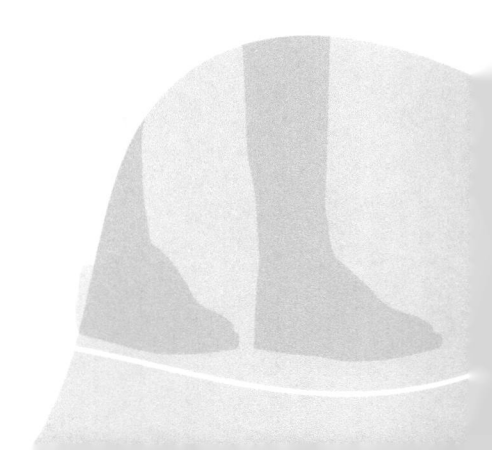

Tortured Soul With A Pen

Free From Your Earthly Burdens

You passed away recently, son
There will forever be an emptiness in my soul
And that will never be filled
A part of my heart that will be forever shattered

I'm trying to find peace in all of this
To say that this is the hardest thing I'll ever do
Is the understatement of my lifetime
I do find some comfort knowing that you will be....

Free From Your Earthly Burdens

Your wheelchair and your illnesses are of what I speak
You're able to fly and be free with all of God's angels

That does bring a smile to my face
Happy tears to my eyes
And some warmth to my soul

My Heart is still shattered, but it is healing

I know you're smiling & laughing more

Flying all around, like when you were younger

Racing around with a towel as a cape

Only now you have wings

Fly with the other Angels, son

I'll see you again one day

And then I'll be....

Free From My Earthly Burdens

Until then, I'll see you in my dreams

And in the clouds

And in my memories

Tortured Soul With A Pen

Thank You For My Birthday Gift, Dad

I want to say thank you
For my birthday gift, dad
Mom took me to the guitar store today
It's exactly the one I wanted

She told me that you bought it
For me a few months ago
And had it held there until my birthday
She said how excited you were to give it to me

I'm wish you were here to watch me open it
Your passing away was so unexpected
I hope you're ok in heaven
Originally, I wanted the guitar to get girls

Now hearing the story behind this gift,
I want to become the best guitar player around
I'll practice everyday
I'll look for the right guys to form a band with

I'm gonna become a musician, dad
Starting today. I'm going right home to learn
I'm gonna improve every day, for you

Thank you again dad
I miss you
I love you

Tortured Soul With A Pen

Tortured Soul With A Pen

DALE

DALE WAS A BIG MAN, WITH AN EVEN BIGGER HEART.
AND AS YOU ALL KNOW, HE WAS MY POPS.
I CAN'T SAY "IS" ANYMORE AND THAT HURTS.

HE MARRIED MY MOM IN 1976,
THEY WOULD BE MARRIED 46 YEARS NEXT MONTH.
THAT MEAN I HAD HIM FOR ALMOST 50 YEARS AND I'M HAPPY WITH THAT.
IN THOSE YEARS HE TAUGHT ME A LOT. BASIC THINGS LIKE HOW TO PLAY BASKETBALL, FOOTBALL, HOCKEY. HE EVEN SHOWED US HOW TO HUSTLE FOLKS IN POOL.

HE TAUGHT ME MORE IMPORTANT THINGS TOO....
LIKE HOW TO TREAT OTHER PEOPLE
LIKE NEVER LOOK DOWN ON ANOTHER MAN, UNLESS YOU'RE HELPING HIM UP.
HE TAUGHT US RESPECT.
HOW TO NOT TALK BACK TO MY MOM. EVEN THO FROM THE OUTSIDE, THAT MAY HAVE LOOKED CHALLENGING, HIS SIZE SORTA MADE THAT EASIER.
HE TAUGHT US FORGIVENESS--MAINLY THRU HIS ACTIONS.
HE TAUGHT US RESPONSIBILITY--BY NOT GIVING US EVERYTHING WE WANTED.

I HAVE FOND MEMORIES OF BEING AT THE COTTAGE WITH MY EXTENDED FAMILY, PAUL, BETTY, JACKIE, ROBERT, JANNETTE AND JENNIFER ALONG WITH THEIR PARENTS. SWIMMING UNTIL OUR SKIN WAS WRINKLED. PLAYING HIDE AND SEEK AT NIGHT. ROASTING MARSHMALLOWS BY THE BON FIRE. PLAYING BOARD GAMES WHEN IT RAINED. PAUL WAS ALWAYS PLAYING CHICAGO AT DINNER TIME....ON THE RECORD PLAYER, IMAGINE THAT. AND DALE WOULD SPIN THE BEATLES.

WE ALWAYS HAD GOOD TIMES ON FAMILY VACATIONS. DRIVING IN THE RAIN, THRU THE MOUNTAINS IN TENNESSE. DRIVING TO TORONTO. SHOPPING TO BUY HIM A JACKET THERE. HE SWORE WHEN HE WAS PACKING THAT HE DIDN'T NEED ONE. WELL, THAT WAS THE FIRST THING WE DID WAS GO GET HIM ONE. WE DID THIS ON A COUPLE OF FAMILY TRIPS.

WE HAD GREAT TIME AT THE MSU FOOTBALL GAMES. WE PLAYED BASKETBALL WITH THE 1979 NCAA CHAMPS...INCLUDING MAGIC. WHO CAN SAY THAT?

HE TOOK ME AND MY FRIEND TO SEE A ROCK CONCERT AND HE HAD A HORRIBLE TIME. BUT WE HAD A BLAST. THAT MADE IT FUN FOR HIM.

WE USED TO CON HIM INTO BUYING THE WEIRDEST BEER SO WE COULD HAVE THE CANS FOR OUR COLLECTION. HE SAID EVERY SINGLE ONE OF THEM WERE HORRIBLE. BUT HE BOUGHT THEM. AND DRANK THEM.... FOR US.

BASICALLY HE WAS EXACTLY WHAT 3 YOUNG BOYS WITHOUT A FATHER NEEDED.
AND I THANK HIM FOR THAT.
HE WASN'T PERFECT, BUT I DARE ANYONE TO SHOW ME BETTER.

AS I SAID IN SOME OF MY WRITINGS, HE WAS THE BLUEPRINT FOR A FATHER. IF I WAS EVER BLESSED WITH CHILDREN, I'D MODEL MYSELF AFTER DALE.
HE WAS MY HERO. NOW MY HERO IS IN HEAVEN.

Tortured Soul With A Pen

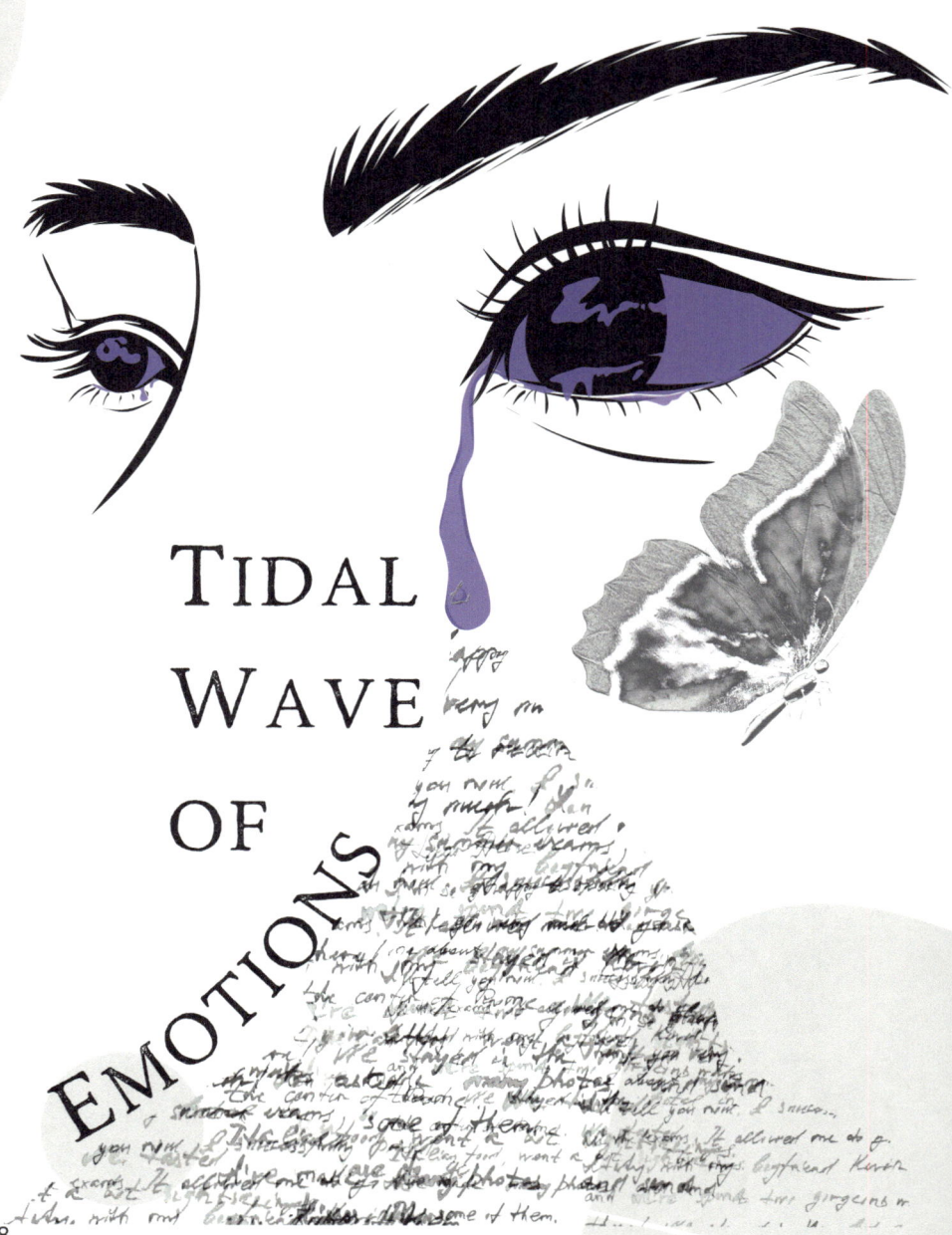

Tidal Wave of Emotions

I SAT DOWN READY TO WRITE.
I SAW THIS CLIP ONLINE THAT TOUCHED MY HEART.
LIKE USUAL, I STARTED WRITING ABOUT IT.

IT'S NO SECRET OR EVEN UNUSUAL
FOR ME TO CRY WHILE WRITING ABOUT PEOPLE.
TODAY WAS A LITTLE DIFFERENT.

THIS STORY QUICKLY WARMED MY HEART.
IT ALSO KNOCKED THE WIND OUT OF MY LUNGS.
I COULD BARELY BREATH AS I CONTINUED TO WRITE.

THE TEARS RACED DOWN MY CHEEKS.
MY NOSE WAS RUNNING
TRYING TO OUTRUN THE WARM TEARS.

I WAS OUT OF BREATH QUICKLY.
I WAS WEEPING AND SNIVELING.

This story began writing itself.
Like my pen was on auto pilot.
I could barely see my tablet.
How did this story hit me so hard?
I don't know these folks.
Then again, I never do.

When I caught my breath,
I looked at my tablet
I was finished.
My favorite piece to date!

I signed my pen name.
Wiped my eyes and nose again.
Then I smiled one of the warmest smiles
That ever crawled across my face.
Thank you for the story.....
You know who you are.

Tortured Soul With A Pen

Tortured Soul With A Pen

WHAT??

21 FROM ONE KID'S GUN.
HERE WE GO YET AGAIN.
ANOTHER SCHOOL SHOT UP.
THE POLICE SHOWED UP.
THEY GOT THEIR KIDS OUT SAFELY.

BUT THEN THEY WAIT FOR SWAT?
FOR AN HOUR?

WHAT??

THEY PEPPER SPRAY THE PARENTS?
HANDCUFF THEM?
KEEP THEM FROM GOING INSIDE?
TO SAVE THEIR CHILD?

WHAT??

THE KIDS CLIMB OUT WINDOWS
ON THEIR OWN?
WHILE A DOZEN OFFICERS ARE OUTSIDE
USHERING THEM TO A SAFE AREA?

WHY DIDN'T THEY GO INSIDE?
AND SAVE THE KIDS?
THEY THOUGHT THE SHOOTER WAS CONTAINED??

WHAT??

HOW WOULD THEY THINK THIS?
NO ONE COULD HAVE CONTAINED HIM.
AFTER ALL, THE COPS WERE ALL OUTSIDE.....

SO THEY SHOULD HAVE ASSUMED HE WAS STILL ACTIVE.
THAT WOULD HAVE BEEN SAFER FOR THE KIDS.
COULDN'T THEY HEAR THE GUNFIRE?

SPEAKING OF "FIRE".
JUST FIRE THEM ALL!
THEY DID NOTHING BUT FAIL THESE 21 TODAY.
THEY FAILED THE FAMILIES, THE PARENTS.

THEY JUST FAILED.
IN EVERY WAY IMAGINABLE.
GO, JUST GO.

Tortured Soul With A Pen

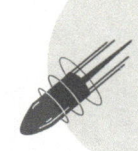

Who Did This To Me

Tires screeching

Burnt rubber

One big loud......

Boom!!!

Followed up with more screeching

The stench of the burnt rubber is fowl

Boom

Crash

Metal on metal

Glass shattering

I flew thru the air

Smashed into a sign

Fell to the ground

Awkward momentary silence

Strange peace

White light

White clothes

Angels

Followed with chaos

Hysteria

Loud chattering and screaming

Crying

Sirens

Commotion

I hear feet pounding on the ground

People screaming...

Can you move?

Are you alive?

Are you ok?

Yes, I responded

I realized what was happening.

Panic hit me

"Yes", I responded again.... "Yes, I'm alive"

I CAN MOVE MY ARMS AND LEGS

MY HANDS AND FEET, EVERYTHING

I CAN MOVE EVERYTHING

I'LL BE OK.

I FEEL TUGGING AND PULLING

THE PAIN IS MASSIVE

I CRY OUT TO STOP

"PLEASE STOP. I'M OK".

"PLEASE"?

"WHY ARE YOU HURTING ME"?

WHY CAN'T THEY HEAR ME?

I WOKE UP IN A WHITE ROOM

MORE VOICES AND CHATTER

NURSES?

DOCTORS?

I'M JUST LYING THERE

NO MORE PAIN

IN FACT, I FEEL NOTHING

All I can do is look around

I can't move

I can't move my legs

My arms

What happened

I was ok lying on the grass

Now I can't feel anything or move any part of me

Who did this to me?

Why?

Why?

Tortured Soul With A Pen

Tortured Soul With A Pen

RACISM

I'm a kind man with a gentle soul.
But I feel your hate
This causes me to hate you.

You need to leave!
Go away!
You're not welcome here!
You never were!

What gives you the right
To judge a man by the color of his skin?
Not the content of his soul.

You are pure evil
Brought here by the Devil.
Designed to disrupt.

To divide this nation.
To divide this world.
You have no place here.

Leave us in peace.
Or we will fight you.
With everything we have.

You can't win.
Love conquers all.

Tortured Soul With A Pen

Tortured Soul With A Pen

EQUALITY

EQUALITY, WHAT AN INTERESTING WORD.
IT DOESN'T MEAN THE SAME TO EVERYONE.

FROM ONE GENDER TO THE NEXT.
FROM ONE RACE TO THE NEXT.
FROM ONE ECONOMIC CLASS TO THE NEXT.

ONE GROUP'S EQUALITY
IS UNFAIR INJUSTICE TO ANOTHER'S.
FOR THEM, IT'S SYSTEMIC DESTRUCTION.

THE PURSUIT OF EQUALITY
FOR THE UNDERPRIVILEGED
FEELS LIKE A REVOLUTION OR
EVEN WAR TO THE PRIVILEGED.

HOW DO WE MAKE
EQUALITY EQUAL?
CAN WE?

SO MUCH DESTRUCTION

I'M YOUNG AND RICH,
I'M ON STAGE EVERY NIGHT.
WOMEN THROWING THEMSELVES AT ME
NIGHTLY BY THE DOZENS.
EVERYTHING I COULD ASK FOR IS AT MY FINGERTIPS.
HOW AM I NOT SUPPOSED TO ABUSE THIS?

NIGHT AFTER NIGHT
DRINKING AND DRUGGING
IT NEVER SEEMS TO WEAR ON ME.
I'VE BECOME A PROFESSIONAL ENTERTAINER, PARTIER AND STUD.

WE'RE OUT OF LIQUOR, IT'S LATE.
WE JUMP IN MY SPORTS CAR AND RACE TO THE LIQUOR STORE.
AS WE FLY UP THE HILL, HAULING ASS.

WE GET TO THE TOP. NO ONE IS ON THE ROAD.......
EXCEPT FOR ONE CAR.
I DON'T REMEMBER COLLIDING WITH IT.

BLUE AND RED HAS ME CUFFED ON THE CORNER.
YOU SAY MY BEST FRIEND IS DEAD
PEOPLE IN THE OTHER CAR ARE SERIOUSLY INJURED.
AND I'M GOING TO JAIL?

CAN I PUT THIS IN REWIND?

THIS IS JUST SOMETHING I CAN'T COMPREHEND.

I LOOK OVER AND SEE MY BEAUTIFUL SPORTS CAR MANGLED.

MY BEST FRIENDS LONELY SHOE NEXT TO IT.

YET, I HAVEN'T GOT A SCRATCH.

YET THIS WAKE OF INJURY AND DEATH BEHIND ME IS MASSIVE.

I DO HAVE ONE NON-PHYSICAL INJURY.

MY HEART IS SHATTERED AND I HAVE HORRIFIC GUILT

I WILL CARRY WITH ME FOR THE REST OF MY LIFE.

LIFE IS NEVER GOING TO BE THE SAME.

UNFORTUNATELY THIS IS NOT GOING TO BE THE LAST HEARTBREAK

OR DEATH IN MY LIFE.

Tortured Soul With A Pen

Tortured Soul With A Pen

I
Want
Us
Back

You rescued me when I was a puppy.
Our bond grew immediately.
Everywhere you went,
I was right next to you.

Over the years,
We became one.
Never being apart for long
Only when you went to work.

Sometimes I got to go there too.
No one could separate us.

Then one day you didn't come home.
Day after day
Night after night.
I felt alone
I felt halved.

What happened?
Did I do something wrong?
Where were you?

Then your mom took me in the car.

We went to the hospital.

You were in a room

Tubes and machines filled the room.

Beeping

Lights flickering.

Everyone took turns petting your head.

Kissing your face.

My turn came last.

I sniffed you

You were different.

You smelled different

Your energy was different

I licked you face

You tasted different.

Your mom petted my head.

And scratched under my chin.

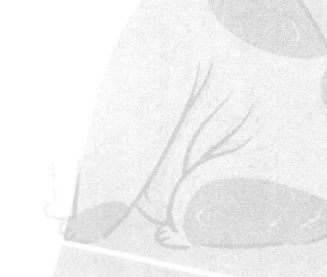

Then the machines lit up

Started beeping

One long flat beep

It just kept going.

Would it stop?

It hurt my ears

You changed again.

You left

You floated up

Up, up and away.

I looked up in sadness

You were gone.

Are you gone forever?

I laid my head on your chest.

I couldn't feel you anymore

You were really gone.

I never knew this day would come.

I wasn't prepared for today.

I want you back.

I want us back.

Tortured Soul With A Pen

If Heaven Had Visiting Hours

WAITING AREA

What an interesting question....

Who could visit?

Immediate Family?

Friends?

How often can one visit?

I know one thing for sure....

I'd visit you every chance they allowed.

I miss you so much it hurts.

I miss you every day.

Please check on the visiting hours for me?

Giving Flowers To The Living

Because you believed in me years ago
Because you gave me my shot
I'm able to take care of my moms.

I brought home enuf money that day
To pay our bills for the next 6 months.
My mom cried happy tears that day.

I am forever grateful to you for that day.
I've made a huge fortune with you since then.
But that was the most important money
I've ever made in my life.
Because it gave my moms peace.

I'll never forget you for that.
Other than moms.
You are the most important figure in my life.

I will repay you in anyway you ever need.

You got it!

I know you don't need money.

But if you ever need me for

ANYTHING?

ANYTHING!

I'm only a phone call away.

I love you like a brother.

I respect you like a father.

I need you like a mentor.

Much love.

Mad respect.

Tortured Soul With A Pen

Uncle Bob Asked For A Job

Police raided the house.
Guns drawn.
Shouting.
As they jumped over a lifeless body.
A young, black boy
Not even a teenager, yet
They thought....
Just another dead black boy
In the ghetto
They must not have cared

Uncle Bob stopped.
Barked at the EMT's
"Save this boy"
They tried.
Nothing.
They tried again.
Nothing.

Uncle Bob, stopped.
Scooped the body up.
It was a child
A 12 year old black child
Bleeding and bleeding.

Uncle Bob was an off duty officer
A white officer in the deep south.

He didn't care about skin color.
About guilt or innocence.
He was gonna save this boy.

He took the boy to the hospital.
Kicked in the door.
Pushed his way to the back
He got the doctors himself.
"Save this boy"
He barked at the doctors.

Uncle Bob was a huge man
They listened.
They worked. Very hard on the 12 year old
They saved him.
The boy grew up and became very famous rapper.
He found Uncle Bob.
Uncle Bob had 2 prosthetic legs.

"Please Uncle Bob
What can I do to repay you?"
Anything, just name it.
You know what Uncle Bob asked for?

Uncle Bob Asked for a job!!!

You Were Right

I ALWAYS SAID HE WOULD NEVER HIT ME.
YOU SAID, EVENTUALLY HE WOULD.
THAT YELLING AT ME WOULD NO LONGER
SATISFY HIS RAGING ANGER.

THE FIRST TIME HE ONLY HIT ME ONCE.
NOW THAT I LOOK BACK,
HE REALLY DIDN'T SEEM THAT SORRY,
HE SAID HE'D NEVER DO IT AGAIN.
HE SAID HE'D GET HELP.

YOU TOLD ME IT WOULD SOON GET WORSE.
THAT HE WAS INCAPABLE OF STOPPING.
HIS HATE AND RESENTMENT WERE TOO HEAVY.
I SAID IT WOULD BE OK.
HE SAID HE'D GET HELP.

YOU WERE RIGHT!

THE BEATING CONTINUED
AND IT WORSENED
MY MAKEUP GOT HEAVIER
SUNGLASSES WERE A REGULAR ACCESSORY.

Anything to hide the evidence

But what about the emotional pain?

You get used to the physical pain.

But the emotional pain never goes away.

You Were Right!

One night he beat me so bad

My neighbor called an ambulance

The doctors told my family

That they lost count on

How many bones are broken.

I don't know if it was the impact of his fist

Or the blood leaking from my face

That turns him on the most

But he seems to get high on it.

He'll never get help.

He's a monster

Monsters don't change!

You Were Right!

Now I lay here in the hospital.
Fighting for my life.
With my kids at my bedside.
Their eyes puffy from days of crying.

They're all prayed out.
It's in God's hands.
Will he finally bring me home to him?

Or send me back down
So my husband can finish the job?

You Were Right!

FIGHT OR FLIGHT

MY OPPONENT STARES ME DOWN

I'M CONFIDENT

YET A LITTLE NERVOUS

IS HE STRONGER?

IS HE BETTER?

IS HE FASTER?

DID HE TRAIN MORE?

THESE THOUGHTS GO THRU MY HEAD

MY COACH SLAPS ME LIGHTLY

DO WHAT WE TRAINED IN CAMP

YOU'LL BE FINE

THIS IS YOUR TIME

YOU GOT THIS

THE BELL RINGS

IT'S TIME

WAR BEGINS

IT'S FIGHT OR FLIGHT
INSTINCTS KICK IN
I PUNCH
I KICK

HE'S HURT

HE'S BLEEDING
HE'S DOWN
THE CROWD CHEERS

THE REF COUNTS TO 10
IT'S OVER
I WON

Tortured Soul With A Pen

Tortured Soul With A Pen

I WAS LOST IN A DREAM

MY IMAGINATION RAN WILD
I PICTURED YOU, ME AND OUR CHILD
I FELL MORE EACH TIME YOU SMILED

YOU WERE THE WOMAN OF MY DREAMS
EVERYTHING I COULD ASK FOR
OR SO IT SEEMS
I WAS YOUR KING,
YOU WERE MY QUEEN.

ONE DAY YOU CHANGED.
MY LIFE WAS REARRANGED.
MY HEART WAS SHORTCHANGED.

YOU WERE NEVER REALLY MINE
MY HEART WAS ON THE LINE
NOW I'M WRITING THIS RHYME

I WAS LOST IN A DREAM
I WAS LOST IN A DREAM

Happily Ever Without

We always thought we'd live happily ever after

The cold truth is, we'll forever be separate.

How did we do this to us?

Why did we do this to us?

Is this how it's going to be?

Unhappily?

Wasn't is supposed to be you and me?

Together?

Forever?

No matter what!

Nothing will get in our way!

Isn't that what we used to say?

How did we become...

Happily Ever Without?

CRASH AND BURN

I DON'T THINK YOU AND I
WERE EVER MEANT TO LAST
WE'RE FROM TWO DIFFERENT WORLDS
WE MOVE DIFFERENT

WE BONDED AND VIBED, YES
WE HAD CHEMISTRY, YES
INCREDIBLE ATTRACTION, YES

UNFORTUNATELY, I THINK WE WERE MEANT
TO CRASH AND BURN
I BELIEVE THIS IN MY HEART

IF YOU LOOK BACK ONE DAY
YOU'LL SEE THIS TO BE TRUE
I THINK YOU'LL ALSO AGREE
IT SURE WAS A HELLUVA RIDE

Tortured Soul With A Pen

EXISTENCE

SINCE THE DAY YOU LEFT,
I'VE JUST BEEN FIGHTING
FIGHTING
FOR MY EXISTENCE!

THE NIGHT YOU PROMISED TO STAY

I WAS ECSTATIC
OVERWHELMED WITH JOY
MY HEART WAS RACING
I ASSUMED YOU MEANT YOU WOULD STAY WITH ME
THAT YOU AND I WERE GONNA GET MORE SERIOUS

I COULDNT HAVE BEEN HAPPIER
THIS IS WHAT I'VE BEEN PRAYING FOR
HOLDING BACK SAYING THOSE 3 WORDS...
WAITING FOR THE PERFECT TIME

WHAT YOU REALLY MEANT WAS THAT
YOU WOULD STAY AWAY FROM ME.
STAY AWAY FOR GOOD.
NEVER TO RETURN AGAIN.
NEVER TO HEAR FROM YOU AGAIN.

MY HEART SHATTERED.
MY EYES RAINED TEARS
MY SOUL WAS DESTROYED
WOW, WAS I WRONG!

Loneliness is My Only Friend

SINCE YOU'VE BEEN GONE,
THE PAIN IS MORE THAN ONE COULD COMPREHEND
IT FEELS LIKE MY HEART WILL NEVER MEND.

SINCE YOU'VE BEEN GONE,
SADNESS IS THE TREND.
LOOKING FORWARD TO THE END.

LONELINESS IS MY ONLY FRIEND.

Tortured Soul With A Pen

ONE WISH

ONE DAY, GOD CAME TO ME
AND ASKED IF
HE COULD GRANT ME ONE WISH,
WHAT WOULD IT BE?
I SIMPLY SAID YOU ALREADY HAVE FATHER....
HE BROUGHT YOU TO ME.

Tortured Soul With A Pen

If There Was No Tomorrow

I ASKED MYSELF ONE DAY.
WHAT WOULD I DO....
IF THERE WAS NO TOMORROW?

I WOULD LOVE YOU HARDER.
I WOULD STRESS A LOT LESS.
I WOULD HOLD YOU TIGHTER.

I WOULD KISS YOU DEEPER.
I WOULD MAKE LOVE TO YOU MORE PASSIONATELY
I WOULD TALK TO YOU NICER.
I WOULD RESPECT YOU BETTER.

I WOULD DO MORE FOR YOU.
I WOULD NOT GET UPSET.
I WOULD BE EVERYTHING YOU COULD ASK ME TO BE.
I WOULD BE SOMEONE YOU'D BE PROUD TO CALL HUSBAND.

I WOULD DO EVERYTHING I SAID IN MY VOWS.
I'D BE THE MAN I PROMISED YOU
I'D BE ON OUR WEDDING DAY.
I'D EARN THE TITLE OF HUSBAND.

Tortured Soul With A Pen

IF
I NEVER
MET YOU

IF I NEVER MET YOU...
I WOULDN'T BE
WHO I AM TODAY.

THANK YOU.

Tortured Soul With A Pen

WIDOW

I NEVER THOUGHT I COULD FEEL THIS MUCH PAIN!

I THOUGHT OF LEAVING YOU.

OR

YOU LEAVING ME

AND HOW THAT WOULD HURT.

BUT YOU BEING TAKEN FROM ME

BUT THIS IS ON A WHOLE NEW LEVEL.

I CAN BARELY BREATHE.

I CAN BARELY FUNCTION.

I FEEL HALVED.

GUTTED AND CORED.

LEFT TO DIE.

WALKING A NEW ROAD ALONE

TODAY IS NOT MY FIRST DAY ALONE
WITHOUT YOU.
BUT MY FIRST DAY OUT OF BED....
WITHOUT YOU.

I'M LOST IN EVERY SENSE OF THE WORD.
I'M IN THE OLD COUNTRY
YOUR OLD COUNTRY.

WE'RE VISITING YOUR FAMILY,
OUR DAUGHTER AND I.
IT'S ALSO MY BIRTHDAY.
MY FIRST WITHOUT YOU.

I'M SO LOST WITHOUT YOU,
YET I HAVE TO GUIDE OUR LITTLE ONE.
THRU THIS TIME OF...
MOURNING.
EMPTINESS.
SADNESS.

GOD I NEED HELP.
I NEED YOU, MY HUSBAND.
I NEED REGULARITY.
I NEED MY OLD LIFE BACK.

I'M WALKING A NEW ROAD.
AND I'M WALKING IT ALONE.

I DON'T THINK I CAN DO IT,
YET, I HAVE NO CHOICE.
OUR BABY NEEDS ME.
HONESTLY SHE NEEDS YOU, TOO
BUT I'LL HAVE TO DO.

EYES PUFFY AND WRINKLED.
SOUL CRUSHED AND DEVASTATED
HEART BLEEDING AND EMPTY.

I FACE THIS NEW ROAD ALONE.
AM I REALLY ALONE?
I HAVE OUR DAUGHTER.
AND I HAVE GOD.
AND I HAVE YOU.
WE'RE JUST A LITTLE DIFFERENT, NOW.

YOU'RE ALWAYS IN...
MY HEART,
MY SOUL,
MY DREAMS.

HELP ME LOVER,
AND I CAN DO IT WITH YOUR HELP.
HELP ME PUT ONE FOOT IN FRONT OF THE OTHER.

HELP ME START ALL OVER AGAIN......

WALKING A NEW ROAD, ALONE

Tortured Soul With A Pen

I'M OUTTA MY HEAD WITHOUT YOU

GRANDMA,

YOUR LOVE WAS UNDENIABLE.
THE KIND OF LOVE NO ONE COULD QUESTION.
YOU WARMED UP THE ROOM WHEN YOU ENTERED IT.
LIKE A RAY OF SUNSHINE-THE PERFECT SHADE OF YELLOW.

YOU WERE THERE EVERY DAY.
YOU NEVER MISSED AN EVENT.
YOU CARED FOR ME NOT BECAUSE YOU HAD TO,
BUT BECAUSE YOU LOVED ME AND BECAUSE I NEEDED YOU.

WHEN I SEE YELLOW, I THINK OF YOU.
WHEN I SEE SUNFLOWERS, I FEEL YOU.
WHEN I THINK OF PURE LOVE, I SEE YOU.

NOTHING COMES CLOSE TO YOUR LOVE.
I MISS YOUR HEART, I MISS YOUR SOUL.
I'M OUTTA MY HEAD WITHOUT YOU.
I'M JUST NOT WHOLE.

AS THE YEARS WENT ON, I LOVED YOU MORE AND MORE.
THIS IS SOMETHING I DIDN'T THINK WAS POSSIBLE.
AND FOR EVERY OUNCE OF LOVE I GAVE YOU,
YOU RETURNED THAT LOVE POUND AFTER POUND.

YOU LOVED ME EVEN WHEN I WAS ASHAMED.

YOU WERE PROUD OF ME WHEN I COULDN'T FACE THE MIRROR.

YOU MADE ME FEEL LIKE A KING WHEN I KNEW I WAS A PEASANT.

I HEARD CHOCOHOLIC THE OTHER DAY AND I THOUGHT OF YOU.

INTERESTING, AS A SELF PROCLAIMED CHOCOHOLIC,

YOU WERE ALSO THE SWEETEST PERSON I'VE EVER KNOWN

NOTHING COMES CLOSE TO YOUR LOVE.

I MISS YOUR HEART, I MISS YOUR SOUL.

I'M OUTTA MY HEAD WITHOUT YOU.

I'M JUST NOT WHOLE.

AS THE YEARS WENT ON, I STRUGGLED AS A GREW UP.

YOU WERE ALWAYS THERE WITH WORDS OF WISDOM

WITH AN EXTENDED HAND TO LIFT ME UP.

YOU BRAGGED TO YOUR FRIENDS ABOUT ME LATER IN LIFE

SOMETIMES I EVEN EARNED IT.

I LOVED PAYING FOR YOUR CABLE TV.
I LOVED TAKING YOU OUT TO DINNER.
I BOUGHT YOU A PEARL NECKLACE, BRACELET AND EARRINGS
MOM SAID YOU ALWAYS WANTED A SET.
I DON'T KNOW WHOSE SMILE WAS BIGGER THAT DAY
WHOSE HEART FELT WARMER.

AS THE YEARS WENT ON,
YOUR BEAUTY NEVER FADED.
LIKE A FINE WINE
BETTER WITH TIME.

NOTHING COMES CLOSE TO YOUR LOVE.
I MISS YOUR HEART, I MISS YOUR SOUL.
I'M OUTTA MY HEAD WITHOUT YOU.
I'M JUST NOT WHOLE.

WE CAME OUT TO VISIT
CHOPPED IT UP FOR HOURS.
NONE OF US WANTED TO LEAVE
BECAUSE WE KNEW THIS WOULD BE
THE LAST TIME WE'D SEE EACH OTHER.

LATER, MOM WAS BY YOUR BEDSIDE HOLDING YOUR HAND.
"IT'S OK MOM, YOU CAN GO, GO BE WITH DAD" SHE WHISPERED
"WE WILL BE OK. YOU TAUGHT US WELL".
SHE SAID IT AND SHE MEANT IT.

BUT GIVEN THE CHANCE,
I'D SELL MY SOUL FOR ONE MORE DAY WITH YOU.
ONE MORE HUG.
ONE MORE TIME
YOU HOLDING MY FACE AND SAYING........
"OH STEVEN DOUGLAS WHAT AM I GONNA DO WITH YOU?"
I MISS THOSE TIMES.
GRANDMA'S LOVE, DOESN'T GET ANY BETTER THAN THAT.

WHEN I HEAR AMAZING GRACE.
I FEEL YOUR HEART
I SEE YOUR FACE.

NOTHING COMES CLOSE TO YOUR LOVE.
I MISS YOUR HEART, I MISS YOUR SOUL.
I'M OUTTA MY HEAD WITHOUT YOU.
I'M JUST NOT WHOLE.

I'M RARELY PROUD OF MYSELF.
I AM PROUD TO BE YOUR GRANDSON.

YOU'RE THE GREATEST WOMAN I'VE EVER KNOWN.
I LOOK FORWARD TO SEEING YOU IN HEAVEN.
I LOVE YOU GRANDMA.

ALWAYS AND FOREVER

J

MY GRANDMA

I SIT HERE SAD AND DEPRESSED.
MISSING YOU MORE THAN I CAN EXPRESS.

I CLOSE MY EYES
I SEE YOU.
I FEEL YOU.
I HEAR YOU.
I SMELL YOU.

I CLOSE MY EYES, REMEMBERING YOUR GRACE.
AS THE TEARS CASCADE DOWN MY FACE .
YES NO WAY YOU COULD BE REPLACED.
FRESH SUNFLOWERS IN A GOLDEN VASE.

I HEAR THE LOVE IN YOUR SWEET VOICE.
I FEEL YOU SQUEEZING MY CHEEKS
I SEE YOUR SPIRIT

IT'S SO PERFECT
GOD I MISS YOU
I WANT TO HUG YOU

BUT I CAN'T
SO I'LL STROLL DOWN MEMORY LANE
HOPING TO EASE THE PAIN.
I DO THIS OVER AND OVER AGAIN.

I'M CONFLICTED
TORMENTED
TORTURED

I'LL HAVE TO WAIT
BUT WAITING FEELS
LIKE TORTUE
LIKE PURGATORY
LIKE A SLOW DEATH.

J

I want to extend a very special thanks to all the people that influenced this book. The people who stories I saw online. The people that I saw in my journey through life. Thank you to all that bought this book. Thank you to all my followers on social media for your feedback and support. Thank you to my friends and family for the support during this process. Without you all, there would be no book.

A very, very special thank you to my editor extraordinaire…. LC Kyng of Kyng Publishings for your proofreading, editing, sketches and cover design. You were a true gift from God. Each volume looks better and better. I'm excited to see what you come up with for Volume Four. Thank you for putting up with my frequent additions, changes and questions. You were incredibly patient and a true angel throughout this process. I could not have done this without you.

♥♥♥♥

Without all of you….
I'd be a
Tortured Soul without a Pen.

Made in the USA
Columbia, SC
06 March 2024